U0564212

第一天去学校

First Day of School

[美]威力·布莱文斯/著　[美]吉姆·帕约/绘

王婧/译

电子工业出版社·

Publishing House of Electronics Industry

北京·BEIJING

本书中文简体版专有出版权由Red Chair Press LLC通过CA-Link International LLC授予电子工业出版社，未经许可，不得以任何方式复制或抄袭本书的任何部分。

版权贸易合同登记号　图字：01-2022-0735

图书在版编目（CIP）数据

第一天去学校 / （美）威力·布莱文斯（Wiley Blevins）著；（美）吉姆·帕约（Jim Paillot）绘；王婧译. -- 北京：电子工业出版社，2023.6
（胖狗和瘦狗）
ISBN 978-7-121-44941-3

Ⅰ. ①第… Ⅱ. ①威… ②吉… ③王… Ⅲ. ①儿童故事 - 图画故事 - 美国 - 现代 Ⅳ. ①I712.85

中国国家版本馆CIP数据核字(2023)第077355号

责任编辑：范丽鹏
印　　刷：天津图文方嘉印刷有限公司
装　　订：天津图文方嘉印刷有限公司
出版发行：电子工业出版社
　　　　　北京市海淀区万寿路 173 信箱　邮编：100036
开　　本：787×1092　1/16　印张：26.25　字数：264 千字
版　　次：2023 年 6 月第 1 版
印　　次：2023 年 6 月第 1 次印刷
定　　价：208.00 元（全 8 册）

　　凡所购买电子工业出版社图书有缺损问题，请向购买书店调换。若书店售缺，请与本社发行部联系，联系及邮购电话：（010）88254888，88258888。
　　质量投诉请发邮件至 zlts@phei.com.cn，盗版侵权举报请发邮件至 dbqq@phei.com.cn。
　　本书咨询联系方式：（010）88254161 转 1862，fanlp@phei.com.cn。

目录

闪亮登场的主角们

克鲁德

艾克

绒球小姐

鲍勃

马丁太太

"鲍勃要去哪里啊？"艾克问。

"他拿着我们的牵引绳呢，"克鲁德回答，"你知道这代表着什么吗？"

"知道，"艾克说，"到了要带鲍勃去散步的时候了。"

"我们这次要去哪里散步呢？"克鲁德问。

"鲍勃喜欢去湖边。"艾克说。

"可是自从你上次把他推进湖里之后，他就不喜欢去了。"克鲁德说。

"那是因为他当时看起来很热嘛。"艾克解释道，"好吧好吧，要不然去公园怎么样？"

"我们也不能去那儿，你不记得松鼠袭击事件了吗？把坚果偷偷放到鲍勃的帽子里，绝对是个馊主意。"

"带鲍勃去散步可真难啊！"艾克感叹道。

"是啊，的确很难。"克鲁德说，"但是我们还是得去，因为鲍勃需要锻炼身体。"

克鲁德和艾克冲着鲍勃叫了起来。

鲍勃上前扣好了他们的牵引绳。

3

　　"快点儿啊，鲍勃！"他们汪汪叫着催促道。克鲁德和艾克拽着鲍勃往人行道走去。

　　克鲁德尽情地享受着新鲜空气。

　　艾克欢快地又蹦又跳，他一会儿在落叶堆里打个滚儿，一会儿边打着喷嚏边汪汪叫着追蝴蝶。就在这时，艾克突然停了下来，抬头向上看去。马丁太太越过围栏看了过来。

　　"那个家伙在哪儿？"艾克急忙问。

　　"这还用问嘛。"克鲁德说。

　　绒球小姐跳上了围栏，她像在舔一根棒棒糖似的轮流舔着自己的两只爪子。

　　"你们好啊，小伙子们。"马丁太太愉快地打招呼，"出来散步吗？"

“你觉得她在看我们吗？”艾克问。

“我觉得没有，”克鲁德说，“我们继续走自己的路就好了。”他拽着牵引绳朝右边走去。

艾克拽着牵引绳朝左边走去：“快点走啊，鲍勃。”

“噢，瞧瞧，”马丁太太说，“他们两个看起来可不太乖呢！你知道他们需要什么吗？”

“需要什么？”鲍勃问。

“他们需要去学校学习一下。”

鲍勃点了点头，表示同意：“这可真是一个顶呱呱的好主意！”

"学校？"艾克说，"我才不要去学校呢！"

"我也不要去，"克鲁德说，"在学校里他们就知道让你坐下。"

"还让你打滚儿。"

"还让你装死。"

"没错没错，"艾克说，"还让我们装死。"他一想到这个就害怕得直发抖。"没门儿，想都别想，我才不要去学校呢。"对艾克来说，这件事儿毫无商量的余地。

失败一次

第二天一早，鲍勃弄来两个小箱子，然后他往每个箱子里面扔了一块骨头。

"喔喔，"克鲁德警告艾克，"你可千万别又上当了。"可是克鲁德话还没有说完，艾克已经跑进箱子里啃起了骨头。

克鲁德忍不住翻了个白眼，"好吧好吧，"他无奈地说，"去就去吧，但是可别想给我们布置什么家庭作业。"说完，他慢慢悠悠地走进了笼子里。

8

狗狗学校外面挂着巨大的广告牌，鲍勃带着克鲁德和艾克走了进去。

一个脸长得又方又扁、鼻子超级超级小的老师迎接了他们。

　　"他看起来可真像一只斗牛犬。"艾克说。

　　"我们的斗牛犬朋友长得可比他可爱多了。"克鲁德小声说。

　　老师指着房间尽头地板上画着的一条由一头一直延伸到另一头的直线。

"我们要干什么呢？"艾克问。

"老师让我们坐在这条线上。"克鲁德回答。

"会不会有生命危险啊？"艾克很紧张。

"这又不是电线，"克鲁德催促道，"快坐下。"

艾克站在线的前面嗅了嗅，又跑到线的后面嗅了嗅，最后站在线上，扭了几下屁股。扑通一声！

"啊哈，这回好多了，"艾克说，"可是，鲍勃要去干什么呀？"

11

　　鲍勃和其他狗主人一起朝着房间的另一头走去。老师站在狗主人们的旁边，当他举起一只手时，房间里充斥着狗主人们呼唤自己狗狗名字的声音。

　　"菲菲！""菲多！""圣诞狗狗！""汪汪先生！""快过来！""快过来！""快过来！"主人们一个个激动地呼喊着。

　　鲍勃也在呼喊着："快过来啊，克鲁德！快到我这儿来，艾克！"

　　艾克歪着头依旧坐在原地，而克鲁德只顾着舔自己的爪子。"我们可比其他的狗狗聪明多了，"克鲁德说，"瞧瞧他们跑起来的样子，他们肯定不会像我们那样训练他们的主人。"

　　鲍勃挥舞着双臂，蹦来蹦去，高声喊："快过来啊，克鲁德！快到我这儿来，艾克！"

　　"这可真是太好玩了，"艾克说，"鲍勃看起来精力十足，他是不是要飞起来了呀？"

　　"我想他是在试着跳舞吧，"克鲁德说，"我们要不要过去呢？"

　　"我都听你的。"艾克说。

　　"再等等吧，"克鲁德说道，"让我们再看看鲍勃还能做些什么。"

鲍勃跳得更高了，喊声也更大了，他飞快地挥舞着双臂，累得脸都憋红了。所有狗狗全都安静地坐在主人身旁，注视着眼前的一幕。

然而，克鲁德和艾克依旧无动于衷地待在原地。克鲁德干脆仰面躺在了地上，嘴里嘟嘟囔囔的，而艾克干脆舔起了地板。

老师指着他们说："失败一次！"

失败两次

"接下来该干什么了？"艾克问，"这可真是太好玩了！"

"也许是魔术表演吧，"克鲁德说，"快看！"

只见那些狗狗主人一个接一个地把自己的手放低，并对他们的狗狗说了句："不许动！"然后他们嘴里就开始叽里咕噜地大声喊着一大串儿词汇："鞋子！太阳！铅笔！书本！"然而他们的狗狗却一动也不动。

"好孩子。"老师对着一只狗狗说道，"一只受过良好训练的狗狗，只有当主人呼唤他们名字的时候，才会有正确的反应。"

紧接着就轮到鲍勃了，他慢慢地把手放低，然后盯着克鲁德和艾克的眼睛说："不许动！"

　　"鲍勃可真是个好孩子，"艾克说，"他学什么都是这么快！"

　　"再等等。"克鲁德说。

鲍勃深吸一口气，然后大喊："鞋子！棍子！腌黄瓜！"

"腌黄瓜？"艾克兴奋地问，"鲍勃带着腌黄瓜吗？"

"好吃的！"克鲁德说。他们飞奔着穿过房间，直接跳进了鲍勃的怀里。

老师皱起眉头："失败第二次。"

"真是太好玩了！"艾克说，"但是下次能来点腌黄瓜就好了。"

这时，鲍勃抱起艾克朝老师走了过去。老师手里拿着一小块展开的紫色床单。

"接下来这个测试，让我们来看看你的狗狗有多聪明。"老师说，"大部分狗狗2~3秒钟后就会从床单底下跑出来。"

鲍勃轻轻地把床单盖在了艾克身上。

"哦哦，好暖和呀。"艾克说着在床单底下扭了扭身子，紧接着他凑近地板嗅了嗅，兴奋地汪汪大叫："我闻到你的味道了，克鲁德！"

"我来了，我来了。"克鲁德摇摇晃晃地朝着艾克走去，然后钻进了床单下面。一眨眼的功夫，这两个家伙竟然蜷缩着打起了盹儿。

"失败第三次！"老师叹了口气。

鲍勃紧挨着克鲁德和艾克，一屁股坐在了地上，"能不能认真点啊，小伙子们。"鲍勃郁闷地说，"你们刚刚是怎么回事儿啊？"艾克把头搭在鲍勃的腿上，透过床单的缝隙向外看去。

"鲍勃好可怜。"艾克说。

"他在学校里可过得不太好。"克鲁德说。

21

终极考验

5

　　"好啦，各位狗狗家长，"老师说，"我们马上要开始今天的终极考验了，现在请把狗狗们带到这条线这儿来吧。"家长们看起来有些紧张，他们按照要求把各自的狗狗带了过去。狗狗们就地坐了下来，个别几只看起来有些不太安分，在那里扭来扭去。

　　艾克翻了个白眼："他们这些家伙，总是那些人让干什么就干什么。"

　　"没错，"克鲁德说，"他们什么时候才能明白，该学习的应该是那些主人嘛，虽然这可能需要花上些时间。"

　　“现在，”老师悄声对主人们说，“让你们的狗狗坐下来然后保持一分钟，哪只狗狗能在规定的时间内保持不动，就算通过测试了。”

　　“我可喜欢坐着了。”克鲁德说。

　　“我能一整天都坐着不动。”艾克吐着舌头。

　　狗主人们半趴在地上，只听房间里的呼喊声此起彼伏："别动！别动！别动！"

　　鲍勃紧紧地注视着克鲁德和艾克，他紧张得汗都流下来了。"别动，"鲍勃祈求道，"千万，千万别动！"

　　"你根本不用拜托我们两次的。"艾克说完躺在地上盯着天花板发起了呆。克鲁德挨着他也躺了下来。

就在这时，马丁太太从教室的窗户外走了过去，绒球小姐就趴在她的肩膀上。绒球小姐一边炫耀地甩动着自己的尾巴，一边不忘冲着克鲁德和艾克哈气。

突然，教室内所有的狗狗开始狂奔，他们大吼大叫，激动地敲打着教室的窗户。教室外的绒球小姐更是弓起了背，哈气声更大了。

　　而克鲁德和艾克呢？俩人依然躺在原地，别说是抬腿了，就是屁股都没有挪过地方，根本就是纹丝不动。"要是他们认识她的话……"艾克说。

　　"是啊，他们就会跟我们一样一动不动了。"克鲁德说。

　　老师把一张上面带有大大的金色星星的结业证书颁发给鲍勃。"简直太神奇了，"老师说，"但克鲁德和艾克确实通过了这次的测试，恭喜他们！"说完，他仍百思不得其解地摇着头走了。

"你准备好回家去了吗？"克鲁德问。

"当然啦，"艾克回答，"不管是什么训练都会让我很头痛，而且鲍勃也很不好训练啊！"

"我有点儿好奇，下次我们教鲍勃点什么好呢？"克鲁德问道。

"让我想一想，"艾克说，"也许我们可以教他叼东西、玩球球、捡棍子，或者吃好多好吃的！"

"真是一个顶呱呱的好主意，哥们儿！"克鲁德说，"那我们赶紧回家，然后开始准备起来吧！"

英文原文

Meet the Characters

Crud

Ick

Miss Puffy

Bob

Mrs. Martin

A Brilliant Idea

"Where's Bob going?" asked Ick.

"He's grabbing our leashes," said Crud. "And you know what that means."

"Yes," said Ick. "It's time to take Bob for a walk."

"鲍勃要去哪里啊？"艾克问。

"他拿着我们的牵引绳呢，"克鲁德回答，"你知道这代表着什么吗？"

"知道，"艾克说，"到了要带鲍勃去散步的时候了。"

1

31

"我们这次要去哪里散步呢？"克鲁德问。

"鲍勃喜欢去湖边。"艾克说。

"可是自从你上次把他推进湖里之后，他就不喜欢去了。"克鲁德说。

"那是因为他当时看起来很热嘛。"艾克解释道，"好吧好吧，要不然去公园怎么样？"

"我们也不能去那儿，你不记得松鼠袭击事件了吗？把坚果偷偷放到鲍勃的帽子里，绝对是个馊主意。"

"带鲍勃去散步可真难啊！"艾克感叹道。

"是啊，的确很难。"克鲁德说，"但是我们还是得去，因为鲍勃需要锻炼身体。"

克鲁德和艾克冲着鲍勃叫了起来。

鲍勃上前扣好了他们的牵引绳。

2

3

"Where will we go this time?" asked Crud.

"Bob likes the lake," said Ick.

"Not after you pushed him in," said Crud.

"He looked hot," said Ick. "Well, what about the park?"

"We can't go there. Remember the squirrel attack? Putting nuts on Bob's hat was a bad idea."

"Bob's not easy to walk," said Ick.

"No, he isn't," said Crud. "But we must. He needs the exercise."

Ick and Crud yapped at Bob.

Bob snapped on their leashes.

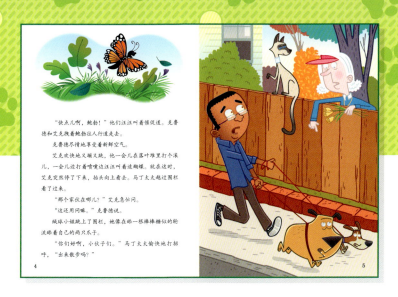

"快点儿啊，鲍勃！"他们汪汪叫着催促道。克鲁德和艾克拽着鲍勃往人行道走去。

克鲁德尽情地享受着新鲜空气。

艾克欢快地又蹦又跳，他一会儿在落叶堆里打个滚儿，一会儿边打着喷嚏边汪汪叫着追蝴蝶。就在这时，艾克突然停了下来，抬头向上看去。马丁太太越过围栏看了过来。

"那个家伙在哪儿？"艾克急忙问。

"这还用问嘛。"克鲁德说。

绒球小姐跳上了围栏，她像在舔一根棒棒糖似的轮流舔着自己的两只爪子。

"你们好啊，小伙子们。"马丁太太愉快地打招呼，"出来散步吗？"

"Hurry, Bob," they barked. Ick and Crud led him onto the sidewalk.

Crud lapped up the fresh air.

Ick hopped. He rolled in the leaves. He sneezed and barked at a butterfly. Then he suddenly stopped and looked up. Mrs. Martin was peeking over the fence.

"Where is you-know-who?" asked Ick.

"Don't ask," said Crud.

Miss Puffy hopped onto the fence. She licked her paws like they were lollipops.

"Hello, boys," she purred. "Out for a stroll?"

"Do you think she sees us?" asked Ick.

"I don't think so," said Crud. "Just keep moving." He tugged his leash to the right.

Ick tugged to the left. "Come on, Bob!"

"Oh, look," said Mrs. Martin. "Those two sure have a hard time on a leash. You know what they need?"

"What?" asked Bob.

"They need to go to school."

Bob nodded. "That's a brilliant idea!"

Miss Puffy hissed a laugh.

"School?" said Ick. "I'm not going to school."

"Me neither," said Crud. "In school they make you sit."

"And roll over."

"And play dead."

"Yeah," said Ick. "And play dead." He shivered thinking about it. "No way. No how. Not going to go." And as far as he was concerned, that was that.

Strike One

The next morning Bob set out two small crates. He tossed a bone into each crate.

"Uh-oh!" warned Crud. "Don't fall for that again." But before he finished, Ick was already inside. Gnawing on the bone.

Crud rolled his eyes. "Fine," he said. "To doggie school we go. But there better not be homework!" And in he waddled.

A big sign hung outside the school. Bob carried Ick and Crud inside.

一个脸长得又方又扁、鼻子超级超级小的老师迎接了他们。

"他看起来可真像一只斗牛犬。"艾克说。

"我们的斗牛犬朋友长得可比他可爱多了。"克鲁德小声说。

老师指着房间尽头地板上画着的一条由一头一直延伸到另一头的直线。

"我们要干什么呢？"艾克问。

"老师让我们坐在这条线上。"克鲁德回答。

"会不会有生命危险啊？"艾克很紧张。

"这又不是电线，"克鲁德促道，"快坐下。"

艾克站在线的前面嗅了嗅，又跑到线的后面嗅了嗅，最后站在线上，扭了几下屁股，扑通一声！

"啊哈，这回好多了，"艾克说，"可是，鲍勃要去干什么呀？"

A teacher greeted them. His face was round and flat. His nose barely there.

"He looks like a bulldog," said Ick.

"Don't insult our bulldog friends," whispered Crud.

The teacher pointed to a line on the floor. It ran from one end of the room to the other.

"What are we doing?" asked Ick.

"The teacher is making us sit on this line," said Crud.

"Does it hurt?" asked Ick.

"It's not electric," said Crud. "Just sit."

Ick stood in front of the line and sniffed. He stood behind the line and sniffed. Then he stood over the line and wiggled his butt. Plop!

"Ah, that's better," he said. "But where is Bob going?"

鲍勃和其他狗主人一起朝着房间的另一头走去。老师站在狗主人们的旁边，当他举起一只手时，房间里充斥着狗主人们呼唤自己狗狗的名字的声音。

"菲菲！""菲多！""圣诞狗狗！""汪汪先生！""快过来！""快过来！""快过来！"主人们一个个激动地呼喊着。

鲍勃也在呼喊着："快过来啊，克鲁德！快到我这儿来，艾克！"

艾克歪着头依旧坐在原地，而克鲁德只顾着舔着自己的爪子。"我们可比其他的狗狗聪明多了，"克鲁德说，"瞧瞧他们跑起来的样子，他们肯定不会像我们那样训练他们的主人。"

12

13

Bob and the other humans walked to the opposite side of the room. The teacher stood beside them. As soon as he raised his hand, the room filled with dog names.

"Fifi and Fido. Santa Paws. Sir Barks-a-lot. Come! Come! Come!" shouted the humans.

Bob yelled, "Come Crud. Come Ick."

Ick sat and tilted his head. Crud licked his paw. "We're so much smarter than the other dogs," said Crud. "Look at how they run. They'll never train their humans that way."

Bob jumped up and down. He flapped his arms. "Come Crud. Come Ick," he screamed.

"This is fun," said Ick. "Look at Bob go. Is he trying to fly?"

"I think he's trying to dance," said Crud. "Should we go to him?"

"I will if you will," said Ick.

"Just wait," said Crud. "Let's see what else we can get Bob to do."

Bob jumped higher. He yelled louder. He waved his arms faster and faster. His face turned a sunny red. All the dogs sat quietly by their humans and watched. All but Ick and Crud. They stayed on the line. Crud rolled on his back and let out a moan. Ick licked the floor.

The teacher pointed at Ick and Crud. "Strike one," he said.

Strike Two

"What's next?" asked Ick. "This is fun."

"Maybe magic tricks," said Crud. "Look."

One at a time, each human lowered his or her hand and said "stay." Then the human started yelling a string of words. "Shoe. Sun. Pencil. Book." The human's dog stayed on the line.

"Good boy," said the teacher to the dog. "A well-trained dog only comes when he hears his name."

Then it was Bob's turn. He slowly lowered his hand. He looked into Ick's and Crud's eyes. "Stay," he said.

"Good boy, Bob," said Ick. "He learns fast."

"Just wait," said Crud.

鲍勃深吸一口气，然后大喊："鞋子！棍子！腌黄瓜！"

"腌黄瓜？"艾克兴奋地问，"鲍勃带着腌黄瓜吗？"

"好吃的！"克鲁德说。他们飞奔着穿过房间，直接跳进了鲍勃的怀里。

老师皱起眉头："失败第二次。"

18

Bob took a deep breath. Then he yelled, "Shoe. Stick. Pickle!"

"Pickle?" asked Ick. "Does Bob have a pickle?

"Yum," said Crud. And the two raced across the room, jumping into Bob's arms.

The teacher frowned. "Strike two," he said.

Strike Three

"That was fun," said Ick. "But next time there better be a pickle!"

Bob picked up Ick. He took him to the teacher. The teacher unwrapped a small purple sheet.

"This shows how smart your dog is," he said. "It takes most dogs only two or three seconds to get out from under it."

"真是太好玩了！"艾克说，"但是下次能来点腌黄瓜就好了。"

这时，鲍勃抱起艾克朝老师走了过去。老师手里拿着一小块展开的紫色床单。

"接下来这个测试，让我们看看你的狗狗有多聪明。"老师说，"大部分狗狗2~3秒钟后就会从床单底下跑出来。"

19

41

Bob gently placed the sheet over Ick.

"Oh, how warm," said Ick. He wiggled under the sheet. Then he sniffed the floor. "I smell you Crud," he barked. "Here I come." He waddled over to him. Crud crawled under the sheet to join Ick. Within seconds both were curled up and snoring.

"Strike three," moaned the teacher.

Bob plopped on the floor beside Ick and Crud. "Seriously, guys," he said. "What was that?" Ick peeked out from under the sheet. He leaned his head onto Bob's leg.

"Poor Bob," said Ick.

"He's not so good at school," said Crud.

The Big Test

"Okay, class," said the teacher. "Here's the big test for today. Put your dogs on the line." The humans did as they were told. They looked nervous. All the dogs sat. A few wiggled and wagged.

Ick rolled his eyes. "They do whatever their human says."

"Yeah," said Crud. "Will they ever learn? It's the humans that need to be trained. And it takes time!"

"Now," whispered the teacher. "Make your dog stay seated for one minute. Any dog who can sit that long passes the test."

"I like to sit," said Crud.

"I can sit all day," said Ick. And he started licking the air.

24　　　　　25

The humans kneeled low to the floor. Chants of "stay, stay, stay" filled the room. Bob looked at Ick and Crud. Sweat dripped down his face. "Stay," he pleaded. "Please, please stay."

"You don't have to ask me twice," said Ick. He rolled over and stared at the ceiling. Crud rolled beside him.

Just then Mrs. Martin walked outside the class window. On her shoulder sat Miss Puffy. She swished her tail from side to side. And she hissed at Ick and Crud.

All the dogs shot across the room. They banged against the window. Growling and barking. Miss Puffy arched her back and hissed some more.

而克鲁德和艾克呢？俩人依然躺在原地，别说是抬腿了，就是屁股都没有挪过地方，根本就是纹丝不动。"要是他们认识她的话……"艾克说。

"是啊，他们就会跟我们一样一动不动了。"克鲁德说。

老师把一张上面带有大大的金色星星的结业证书颁发给鲍勃。"简直太神奇了，"老师说，"但克鲁德和艾克确实通过了这次的测试，恭喜他们！"说完，他仍百思不得其解地摇着头走了。

Ick and Crud didn't move. Not a foot. Not an inch. Not even an eensy-weensy centimeter. "If they only knew her," said Ick.

"Yeah, they would have stayed with us," said Crud.

The teacher handed Bob a certificate. It had a big gold star on it. "I don't know how," he said. "But Ick and Crud passed the test. Good luck with them!" He shook his head and walked away."

45

"你准备好回家去了吗？"克鲁德问。

"当然啦，"艾克回答，"不管是什么训练都会让我很头痛，而且鲍勃也很不好训练啊！"

"我有点儿好奇，下次我们教鲍勃点什么好呢？"克鲁德问道。

"让我想一想，"艾克说，"也许我们可以教他叼东西、玩球球、捡棍子，或者吃好多好吃的！"

"真是一个顶呱呱的好主意，哥们儿！"克鲁德说，"那我们赶紧回家，然后开始准备起来吧！"

Are you ready to go home?" asked Crud.

"I am," said Ick. "All this schooling is giving me a headache. Bob's not easy to train."

"I wonder what we can teach him next?" asked Crud.

"Hold the doggie door," said Ick. "Maybe we can teach Bob to fetch. Balls. Sticks. And lots of food."

"Good idea, buddy," said Crud. "Let's go home and get started."